REWRITING THE BODY

Also by Wyatt Townley

Poetry

The Afterlives of Trees

The Breathing Field

Perfectly Normal

Nonfiction

Yoganetics: Be Fit, Healthy, and Relaxed One Breath at a Time

Kansas City Ballet: The First Fifty Years

DVD

Yoganetics: Relaxation and Basic Workout

Rewriting the Body

Wyatt Townley

Stephen F. Austin State University Press

For information:
Stephen F. Austin State University Press
PO Box 13007, SFA Station
Nacogdoches, TX 75962
sfapress@sfasu.edu;
www.sfasu.edu/sfapress
936-468-1078

For information on discounts for bulk purchases:
Texas A&M University Press consortium
www.tamupress.com
800-826-8911

Cover and book design: Sarah Denise Johnson
Cover art: Matt Manley, "vas hermeticum"
Author photo: Terry Weckbaugh

Printed in the United States of America on acid-free paper

Townley, Wyatt
Rewriting the Body / Wyatt Townley
ISBN: 978-1-62288-216-8

forever for Roderick
and Grace
and for my students: my teachers

...and your very flesh shall be a great poem and have the richest fluency not only in its words but in the silent lines of its lips and face and between the lashes of your eyes and in every motion and joint of your body. . .

—Walt Whitman, 1855 preface to *Leaves of Grass*

CONTENTS

REWRITING THE BODY

I. Open House

It's Easy

to enter the room
of this poem. Less
so to stay. But do

until this line
ends and begins
again, dropping

to the next stanza.
If you're still here,
have a drink, have

the run of the place,
whatever you like
in the right glass. Clink!

And the view—take
your pick: an ocean
under a stick of moon,

or this one I've got
at the edge of the woods
in the softest rain

that hangs off the undersides
of branches, each drop
holding a world

about to fall. And when
it does, it isn't
gone. Inside this book

are other rooms,
a whole house curled
inside a tree. I'll leave

the porchlight on.

Knowing the Difference

The porchlight is on
its gold pours down
around your ankles

it follows you up the curve of night
slides through rows of corn
behind the parking lot

and when you have forgotten

the porchlight is on
the glossy black back
of the waterbug under the welcome mat

on the soundless
harp of the spider
behind the downspout

when you have not found what you had

to lose and your steps
are slow with doubt
the porchlight is on   look down

at your old shoes gleaming
you're the door you're
the difference between in and out

Sweeping the Porch

Some of the bugs were leaves
some of the leaves were stains
some of the stains

cannot be swept away

they were lying
there before you

were on your own
hands and knees scrubbing
will not cure them

a stranger

who no longer has hands
to sweep this porch
has reached you nonetheless

beneath your feet

BLACK WEDDING TRAIN

behind my back the back-
yard a black wedding train
made of catshit weeds and mud

in its folds boys
circle a girl
facedown in the dandelions

the ants bear witness
to her fisted silence
and the zipper's long scream

birds fall out of the sky
night falls rain then years
behind the bride

black wedding train so heavy
shushing and clanking
tin cans and trash bags

get off get out disband the choir
this wedding train
is trimmed with razor wire

One Way

Descend: The poem is both
basement and
torna-
do

.

The Closet

villanelle

The shoes lead here—all shoes show up at night
and call it a day. Each one points back to you.
Step in, step out of town and out of sight.

The shoes line up in rows, with toes upright—
the Birkenstocks, spike heels, and combat boots.
The shoes lead here—all shoes show up at night.

The ruby slippers and the red shoes might
join forces in a rowdy pas de deux.
Step in, step out of town and out of sight.

Did twelve disciples get into a fight
or twelve dancing princesses get screwed?
The shoes lead here—all shoes show up at night.

Step by step you've circled back to write
your memoirs in a closet rendezvous.
Step in, step out of town and out of sight.

The shoes line up in rows with toes upright
above or underground—a grave debut.
The shoes lead here. All shoes show up at night:
Step in, step out of town and out of sight.

SHELTER

the smallest room
in the house
is mine
its lock shines

from where I sit
everything is shining

the tiny hexagons
that march with linked elbows
at my feet
will carry me away

from my small days
and big secrets big
as the backyard

a gang of boys
in a ring bigger
than this room bigger
than a mother and a father
whose ears were four helmets

four being the end   boom
of childhood over and out
and I have found myself

at home at any age
in the world's smallest rooms
where I can turn

a lock like a corner
of this page

THE FITTING ROOM

Remove clothes
kiss the sky

goodbye enter
at your own risk

threading your life
through a hole

in the water
precisely the size

of your body
going down

further down
your last breath

the blue thread
from the known

to the never
known new

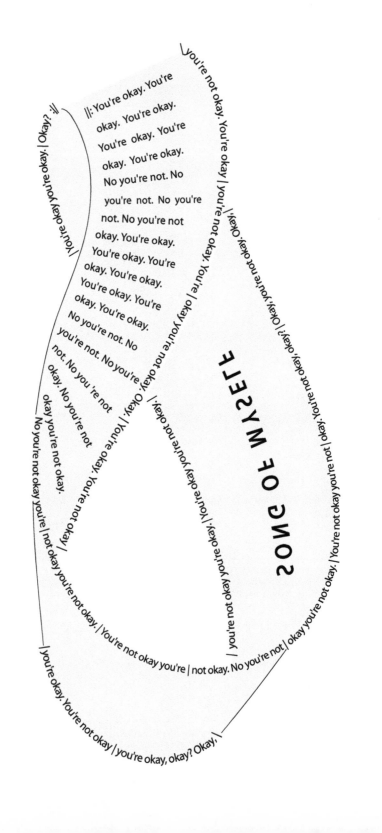

II. Meanwhile You

One House

Before we could meet across the room
a thousand miles from here
with a dozen years between us
we would have to learn to count
on what wound its way
from the feet up the turning

staircase of the spine and out the mouth
because the feet kept running
from what the mouth was saying
then the mouth would run
on and on while the feet stayed put

and isn't this the project of a lifetime
to live in one house

bounding up from the basement
feet and gut and heart and head
together up the wooden stairs
to the first floor and the second
where the view opens out
and a squirrel on a branch
freezes   his eye on you

whatcha gonna do now
whatcha gonna do

Behind the Shirt

My nipples have eyes.
They are watching out

for my heart, bouncers
at the door. They're not

picky. They don't see
shit, can't count fingers

in front of them. They
strain against the shirt

for a view, noses
through a chain-link fence.

They've had enough
of the backs of things—

bras, the insides
of hands and mouths.

They need space, they
need air. Chuck the blouse

and underwear. Their
tiny faces wrinkle, ages

younger than the stars
they wait for. Till then,

they toughen up, pretend
to guard the door.

Meanwhile You While He

1
the architect

Meanwhile, you'd have shivered
writing on the side
porch in the woods. You would

have run from the polished
rooms he kept to perfection
your desk banished

out of sight among the trees,
space heater at your ankles
and flapping plastic

taped over the view.
The house was small, but you
were smaller still. You turned

sideways and vanished on a hill
while he in photos circles
celebrities, his fingers wrapped

around the stem of a glass, an arm
around the waist of the latest
namebrand, his not yours.

You there in the mossy woods,
while he on a glossy
page the tree fell for.

2
the musician

Meanwhile, you'd have stepped
over his blond body.
What a crime, what a trail

of bottles from the porch
to the fridge to the floor—
porch to fridge to floor...

but between the bases, poems
in Greek and thirsty French
kisses, buttons undone, you in one
arm, guitar in the other, and the music
he made would make you
a river straight to the grave.

Who'd have gone first,
now neither, both

alive at a distance—
him singing in the shade
at a country fair, while
you behind a podium
or scribbling in your chair.

3
the actor

Meanwhile, you'd have burned
alive in his eyes as he offered
you a light—offering light!—

or lightning. You withdrew
your hand from the fire,
but not the heat. Late night
you saw him on TV where years
redrew his face. These days

he spreads himself on billboards
while you unroll your yoga mat
learning to disappear. You've
changed—you're thriving, dear.
In your dreams he would drive

your car off the road. It burst
into flames, but you escaped
to see his ashen face, and rise
to ride three decades from that place.

4
the stockbroker

Meanwhile you'd have gone
hungry thirsting for
substance in the absinthe.

His goal was smoothness
in all things. And so he was—
tallblondandhandsome

with a voice that unrolled
for eighty-two miles
from New York to New Haven,

a Yalee named Rome,
who could rearrange a room
by walking through.

You turned his head.
He turned his back
when you turned home.

5
the accountant

Meanwhile, you'd have left
him alone. *What's wrong
with this picture?*

You open your closet:
the blazers buttoned
like they never were,

[handwritten: accountant]

the dresses zipped
like they'd been to church—
and the smell of his cologne.

He liked tall women,
women just his size.
He was debonair.

When he got into your
clothes, he preferred
you weren't there.

[handwritten: Surprise]

6
the writer

Meanwhile, how we moved
through the crowd of unusual suspects
goodbye after goodbye,

rehearsing to meet eyes
across a room betrayal and art
had brought us to.

I spilled the wine
and you dropped to wipe it up, the start
of a consecrated life.

In thirty years we've birthed
a shelf of books and a singular child,
her signature midair

with every breath,
every night closer to the unknown
reader in the lamplight.

REJECTION SLIP

- ☐ Does not meet our needs at this time
- ☐ Try back in a couple hours
- ☐ Too long for our taste
- ☐ Too short for our taste
- ☐ We have no taste
- ☐ Too deconstructionist
- ☐ Too reconstructionist
- ☐ Reminds editor of old boyfriend
- ☐ Get over here right away
- ☐ Best of luck placing your manuscript elsewhere
- ☐ Get a wastebasket
- ☐ Get wasted
- ☐ Go back to school
- ☐ Go back to bed
- ☐ Thank you for thinking of us
- ☐ After careful consideration
- ☐ You've got to be kidding

Eclipse
for William Merwin

Impossible to lose
your sight

that saw and saw through
the professors whose

mouths were always moving
the politicians

whose fingers
pointed only at others

the women who fell over
and over into the blue

eyes of the poet
who has entered the dark

swaying of palms
under a smear of stars

all you can't unsee unsay
each syllable burned

into the night
still shining the way)

THE LIBRARY

In the dark pockets
behind our knees
we hold whole books

see how they open
and close as we cross
the subway platform

folding the blur of Broadway
the shush of the empty stage
into muscle memory

bending and straightening
closing and opening
recording the cornfield

the mountain and every flight
of stairs we devoured
on the way to each other

in the secrets of knees
these creaking and clicking
autobiographies

in which is written nothing
less than the history
of recorded time

we had together
a few decades under a tree
a child now swings from

Mal de Débarquement

It's not as if the world
swirled, dizzy
from the spin, like a girl

in the grass who'd been twirling
too long. It's an inside job.
Not visual: *visceral.*

The day unrolls. Underfoot
it's a tilting Titanic
while the sky stays put.

The room sways. Rugs
rise and subside
under our chairs. The waltz

we've fallen into
climbs the ocean's
churning stairs. Just talking

while rocking is more
than I can manage
long since the ship's

ashore. What did you say?
You're waving. You're
moving your lips.

WALKING WATER

Inside us the ocean
sways like a cradle
in which we rock   rock

and are drawn like the tide
to the moon twice a day
we carry our water and it carries us

we are a good pail with legs
foot by foot on the turning
mountain of the world

water walking on the prairie
walking water on the road
up the stairs through a door

where the view rushes out of us
through the window to the woods
rushing water in the desert

rushing water in this chair
and that one you're in
water walking

and what is solid is not at all
what we thought   the rock
worn away by the rocking

First Kiss

Here you are forty years
later in a white coat
examining my ears.

All I can think
is how your tongue once
turned in the tunnel

you're peering into. The
fault is not in my ears,
but *between* them!

No one can see that far.
But could we gaze back
through the years and dead stars

to the doorstep of my parents' house,
you bending down with your tall mouth
to make the softest landing on mine,

having thrown off my balance
so tenderly, can you explain,
good Doctor, how to regain it?

DRIVING KANSAS

What sticks up
sticks around.
Grain elevator, water tower, steeple.

Elevator,
tower,
steeple.

Towns slide by, parades
of telephone poles—
the voices they carried,

silent. The stone bank's a tomb
by the post office, the letters
and the hands that wrote them,

elevator,
tower,
steeple,

gone. We are the last
letter sent here. All week
we arrive and arrive.

The rest goes like cursive,
like rain into earth—the natives,
the neighbors, the porch.

MORNING COFFEE

We're drinking the sky
sip by sip

it's going down
to the bottom of our cup

we fill it up
lean into the brown

liquid like Narcissus
out of the blue

clouds slide in
to kiss us

if we linger at the lip
looking down

to see up
we do it for the view

that drip by drip
moves through

NIGHT WINE

At the bottom
of the glass

lies the moon
a girl

on a swing
at the end

of the wine
is the end

of the road
the last thing

seen
is the sky

going down
her throat

WEDDING DRESSES

They whisper across childhood,
across the endings of stories
and centuries. We put them on
as our young mothers did
dipping our toes into pools
of moonlight one foot at a time
through the four generations
and seven veils of being.

One zip and they hug us
the way cars do cliffside,
turning and tucking toward the mountain.

The slippers go under with no sound
like the feet of ducks paddling
beneath the pond's perfect mirror.
Brides have no feet, mermaids
of light gliding down an aisle
toward the kiss. We slide off

into night, swelling
and collapsing into scenery.
But the dresses outlast us.
They whisper in their caskets
in the corners of attics
and basements of sold houses.

On another day in another year
a girl will come upon them
at the back of the closet
and in their stored and storied glow
enter the fold.

ADVICE

for Grace and Spencer

All I can say
is what the wedding gown
whispers to the lawn

is what winter is
telling summer
under the shoes of the groom

the cat says it best—
or eventually—
purring

and nothing says it better
than the breath
of the one in bed beside you

what would I say on your wedding day
but the sound of wind in trees
the rising of hair on the arms

Thirty Years

have crossed the table
since I looked down
then back at you

in the candlelight
the first sip
of wine at my lips

whatever we were about
to say now rises
in our throats the same

words we know better
than our name
while hair went white

across a table we're
still mid-prayer
mid-bite

III.   *When the Diving Board Ends*

PENTIMENTO

Behind this view
is another view.
Under this painting,

another. Before the trees
we planted, before
the leaning wheat,

before the bluebird moved
into her box
and the white moth

ticked at the window,
before this house
was another house.

Behind this country
is another country.
Bison and smoke

signals in the wince
of an eye. Before
the corn, the floor

of an inland sea.
From water to earth,
earth to air, the wind sorts

it back, blows it forward
like the pages of a book.
Behind this book

is another book.
The narrative descends
into mystery, the characters

amend their names.
Who's behind the eyes
to take it in?

Behind this body
is another body.
It is made of sky,

and it changes its stripes
from black to lilac
blue to red to black again.

It was always you
behind me, you
behind the pen.

THE FAILING HEART

It's what we've hung our hat on
our every breath strung to it
arms and legs its dangling dummy

it's what our ribs are ribbons for
circling the maypole
and it's going under

undergoing what we haven't
it's the unheard backup
singer in the dark

the pulse of the poem
snapping its impudent fingers
in the bottom drawer

as we shuffle off to what
was important before
someone's head hit the floor

Leaving Home

Like a girl slipping out of her clothes,
I'm leaving home, this mobile home:
head, shoulders, knees and toes, knees and toes...

and eyes and ears and mouth and nose.
I combed my hair; I leave my comb
behind, a girl slipping out of her clothes.

Wherever I have gone, the body goes.
Breath by breath, it writes its poem—
head, shoulders, knees and toes, knees and toes.

Two breasts, new hips, an old story. I suppose
all books must end—but what a tome,
this girl slipping out of her clothes.

It's poetry in motion—or is it prose?
What finally held it up was chrome
and head, shoulders, knees and toes, knees and toes.

As yoga always finishes with corpse pose,
we drop the body, a drape of bones
like a girl slipping out of her clothes—
head, shoulders, knees and toes, knees and toes.

A PERFECT DEATH

"You have a perfect life," said
the guest. And the perfect
house. Yes, the perfect spouse

from under a perfect rock.
We are crawling out together
on the side of this perfect cliff.

We are very slow. It hurts only
a little as the knee slides off,
a hip, and finally, the heart. If

losing is an art, as Bishop said,
we're perfecting it, dropping
a suitcase here, an infant there,

a funnel through the perfect air,
crusts of bread on a rising trail
that could end up anywhere—

under this bush, at the top
of that tree. Or in bed.
Our perfect bed. We like it there.

We've thumped and howled
and slept our perfect way as far
as I can tell. And now

the howl of the coyote
is our lullaby, the owl's cry
our doorbell.

In Extremis

after Mary Oliver

You do not have to be
good. You do not have to

eat what is given. You do
not have to get up.

You do not have
to quiet down or change

your gown. You have
only to breathe—take

the whole room
into the hallways

of your lungs and let
it out—the house

rearranged one breath
at a time. Just breathe.

Then do it again.

Nothing but Everything

Will it be good or bad—the news
when you're by the telephone
with nothing but everything to lose?

It's the call you won't refuse.
You double-check the dial tone.
Will it be good or bad—the news?

Make lunch, pick up a book, or snooze
the day away before it's known
if there's nothing/everything to lose.

Why call it fair or foul? Choose
your point of view before the phone
announces, good or bad, the news.

Not bad *or* good—that's just reviews.
Or "it's all good." Or it's foreknown.
Everything's nothing, win or lose.

So play, you dogs. Nevermind who's
busy carving your headstone.
Neither good nor bad, the news.
Everything but nothing to lose.

WAITING FOR THE CALL

Today the trees are loud
between the cardinals, owls,
chickadees, the yowl
of something small with fur,
wind in the hands
of the cottonwood, squirrels'
commotion overhead.

A girl can hardly think.
She steps outside for rest
from what's inside. Everything's
talking at once. Except
the phone—just lying
there!—her brother on a bed

post-op, tubes flowing
from the holes they made in him.
Now only birds make their calls,
and the neighbor's dog
repeats what's just been said.

And said. Life and more life, still
the phone plays dead.

Force of Nature

Agree with the river.
Agree with the field
and the tree. If you agree
with the wind that rises
in the midst of your life
running through everything,
rearranging the best
laid plans, branches down,
leaves scattered, you will agree
with what's under your feet.
There are your parents.

The Blue Hat

The forecast was wrong.
The bald guy smiling
and wrong. The blonde
with swinging hair

wrong. Their software,
their reading of currents. Rain,
they said, rain for days.

We wore the wrong shoes,
postponed the garden,
the walk in the woods.
Overhead: blue—and red-

tailed hawks make their arcs;
sun and wind cross
in a tango of shadows.

The forecast was wrong.
And that prognosis?
The doctor sat down.
We had the chat.

Now lose the umbrella
for the big blue hat.

The Lesson

A girl needs a teacher
she walks into the classroom
of the woods

the trees advise her
to grow down
she spends her life falling

all day each night
the wind assigns
its infinite homework

the years inscribe
their lectures in her scars
and when she finds

she can walk no further
she plants her heart
in the earth

and children climb
into her arms

Why Sleep is Round

from the curve of the sun

that spun us here

to the curve of the earth

to the curve of our bones

to the curve of our breath

from the arch of the spine

born from the turn

toward one another

that came before

the long swerve home

we round another corner

down the back of the night

from the curve of the moon

again we return

to the curve of the mother

ship to shore

Defending the Fort

We are giving way
between our bones

the logjam in the hip
the dam in the back

of the waist a space
in the shape of pain

we are only beginning
to lay down arms

the tiny forts
we held for years

their toothpick flags
staking claim

on the landscape
the moment we stop

defending is the same
moment it's ours

MOVING EVERY TREE

You're disappearing. Behind
the folds of your eyelids
I can't find you.

You toddle down the hall
in your old coat. In your slippers
stands a woman I don't know.

On your yoga mat a stranger
bends and straightens your knees.
She is breathing for you until you return.

Not even in your arms
do I find you. You've gone out
the window down the downspout

into the distance. It's Spring.
You're somewhere circling a bonfire
under a star-strewn sky.

The wind moves every tree
searching for you.

Snow Angel

She's nowhere everywhere.
Your mother's hems
catch in the branches, beaks

of birds, peaks of houses.
Now the sky lets out
the weather she held back—

an avalanche of blizzards,
thunder and snow, thunder
and snow. She's mid-air all over

town, underfoot in every yard.
She's in your hands. Make a snowball,
throw as hard and far as death. Lie

down, make an angel. She's behind
your back as you open and close
your arms, your legs…your throat.

Fold her in, let her out mid-breath
in a cloud. Forgive the ghost
that lives inside your coat.

Lumbar Garden

In the lumbar garden
weeds spring up flowers
die down
a rose unwinds and flies
to the ground

its petals settle
into mud
underwhich
roots link elbows
unknown to the bud

more growth more
loss move
together in the stem
the taller
the bloom the longer

the fall   when
bugs come feasting
on what remains
their little legs stir
and turn the world

behind the waist
years leaves rain
into the earth
in the lumbar garden
underdeath birth

A CHANGING VIEW

The birds are circling, searching for the nest
they built last week, but now the tree is gone,
and so the view has changed. Who says less

is more? Notice how the squirrels are stressed,
halting at the stump, zigzagging the lawn.
The birds are circling, searching for the nest,

and so are we. Every night we undress
and blunder into bed with a weary yawn.
While the view has changed, we love no less.

We lose some hair, we lose some weight, and yes,
our bearings in the hours before dawn.
Like birds we're circling, searching for the nest

that marked our place in the sprawling wilderness
of years, and all we've bravely undergone.
The view keeps changing, changing. We're breathless

flying to that long-lost first address
whose long forgotten porchlight's always on.
The birds are circling, searching for the nest.
Our view will change again—to limitless.

After You Died

I breathed

the long black sleeve of night
down my throat and pulled it
down my spine down my legs

closed my eyes and went under
the covers breathed it down
again and again as if its starry buttons

could stub a path to you

I kept breathing down the dark
silence you left
in which I am trailing

the hems of your last breath

Day After

The light will change the day
after. Cars will follow

the road, paint
by number, curving left,

curving right between the lines.
The stars

stay over the house
when you're inside, over

the clouds when you're out.
Look. It is going

to rain. Everything
will shine again.

And you there breathing
above this book

will close it
and rise into your life.

moving still still moving moving still still moving
moving still
moving still still
moving moving
still still
moving moving
still still moving
moving still still
moving moving still
still moving moving

still still moving moving still
still moving moving still still being
still being and being still
still being and being still moving
and being moved being still
being moved and being still
and being moved and still being moved
beyond being and moving beyond
moved beyond being and moving beyond

moving beyond
beyond being
being beyond
beyond being
being beyond beyond

being being
beyond beyond
being beyond and
being back
being beyond
and being back
back beyond being still
moving

68

QUITTING TIME

The actors scrub their faces
and go home. The cook unties

the apron. The crook puts down
the gun. Everywhere people

are stepping out of their shoes,
setting down their backpacks.

Briefcases line the cornfields,
piles of jackets and ties and

upturned high heels. Stop
the car. Get out, get off

the phone. You're being called.
Empty your hands.

When the diving board ends,
keep singing.

IV.   Rewriting the Body

Rewriting the Body

Fadeup in three
two
1
It arrives and you turn it
            around and around
            you pass it
to another
            take it back
            like a hand from the fire
you set it down
            pick it up
            while decades slide
through the mailslot
            their bills past due
            until you come home
finding a poem
            in your back pocket

2

                                             Places please
                                             House to half
                                             Kill the house

Your Dream Home says the sign

The astonished gate
a loose tooth
through which you thread
your long late youth
unsure of what
you'll find   and won't
                   chills up the back
                       of the legs
                               Cue 1: Warning
                                 Cue 1: Go

Sold As Is
Inspections Welcome

First   what's not there
no clothesline   no swingset
no sandbox   no roses   no picnic
table   and what is   a chain
link fence around the overgrown

backyard where one life ended
someone else's began
your childhood yanked
from you beside the roses

under the walnuts
in front of the sandbox
the swings still moving

as the boys circled up
and pulled down your pants

You remember the ants

Blackout

3
Here's where it ends
return to the spot
the music stopped
your small legs a wishbone
behind the Dream Home

chills up the back
of the arms

A lifetime later   you step
into the grass   no tree topples
no storm spins up   just you there

kneeling   the smell of earth
somewhere   a car honking
NEEDS MINOR COSMETIC REPAIR

On another street   on another day
you will sing of this   the walnuts fling
their black hats   to your feet

4
It takes a lifetime
          to find the feet

the ones that didn't
          run

to come upon
          them   strike

up a conversation
          the long

lost friends you never
          knew lived

down the block
          now they reply

with every step
          closer toward away

but by that very
          day you have walked on

5
Do you wanna dance

Curtain up
Cue music

At the bottom of the dark
    a chord is flung

Go lights
Fadeup in three
two one

Gold dawns down the arms
    spills onto the stage
your spine unrolls into lights
    that blind you never
look directly at the sun
    spot the exit and run
your long hair trailing
    in the wind that motion makes
the music's golden leash
    turning you the world
swirling sweat spinning
    off your brow your feet
hopscotching Fibonacci's
    pattern off the stage
and into sunflowers the curls
    of waves and the shells they carry
scaling the scaffolds of galaxies
    until they know
the way to now

Fadeout in three two one

    beginning with a bow

6
If you feel physically
as if the top of your head
were taken off

you know

it's so easy to lose
your place in the open-
ended story of your life

that is poetry

written in the hillside of your hip
and the valley of your waist
in the corners still unkissed

poetry

in the through line
between this step and the next
and every time you breathe

you know that

to turn a page
first you gotta
open your fist

Cue husband
Husband: go
Cue child
Child: go
Cue decades

7

Letting go of time
your hands open
hours fall out weeks

pour onto rocks
boots test the slope
but can't find a foothold

—think—

So this is how
we age
behind our backs

a path of years
our tracks
covered with words

—blink—

in a month you are
still sitting
over this page

8

The cane on the lip
of the stage

finds the curb   she
who swam the air

crunches gravel in the hip
Ave Maria   Gratia Plena

a clatter of bones amid
the holy poetry of the everyday

the tea kettle and the siren
the child and the owl

paired through the ears into
the music of a life-

time crossing
stageright to stageleft

the first cry
and the penultimate

a bowing of strings
and a string that breaks

at last the violin
lands on the high wire

underlined by cellos
then silence

turns the room
like a woman's dress

when she leaves you
                    at the treeline you are waiting

9

Places
House to half
House to black

Deep in the forest of the dream
trees hold you close in their dark chair
the heat shakes with cicadas
in the vibrato of midair

your limbs fleshed out on a gurney
your colours wet under the brush
the scalpel the pen the painter
the doctor looking for what

is worthy of the gesture
now that the landscape has torn
the river running under bone and bridge
to every crevice and the long deserted "if

only" running from the dead
through us to the unborn
and out of sight   up ahead
the waterfall   the cliff

10

Sound go

The man at your ear
is telling you a story
whose words are the rain
entering the green
jungle of your fear
you bloom into dream
downstreamdownstream
then wake to his words
falling in rivulets
where creekside you
have wandered every night

since unremembered youth
among the fallen branches
of trees that are dying
to know you again

Fly the scrim

11
Night folds its blue curtain
    light climbs
down the trees its hand
    on the back of your waist
showing the way
    to the day finding an aisle
seat between dreams and
    the chickadees'
two notes   here
    and a whole step down

12
    "Matter accounts for 4 percent of the universe's mass."
        —The Associated Press

Go lights
Fade up in three
two one

That's you that's me
the chipmunk and the juddering
fridge in the kitchen

It's the hum
of traffic over the shoulder
and the woods through which
you aim your gaze

It's the bird that swings
on invisible ropes from
tree to tree it's the knee
crossed over another knee
and the pencil crossing
the page like a wave to shore
coming back for what

at its tip is
the sound of wind

It's the next of kin
and the book these words
have hopped into and the chair
that surrounds you it's what
unfurls out your window
at the distant end of your stare
it's beyond that across an ocean

Waves go
Cue lights
Downpool go

It's an elbow into which
someone leans over coffee
closing her eyes to remember
the boy who stroked her face
with his lips and it's the boy
who has not forgotten
though he never thinks of her
and lives in a country
she cannot pronounce

It's the nouns
it's the stars
we point to with our bones

It's the stones
that people are holding
yelling and chanting
and a woman who has fallen
beneath their feet
closing her eyes for the last time

It's the wine

It's the twenty
kids on the red
floor of a classroom
their small hands curled
into shells

It's the bells
that fill our ears it's
the moon that pours
its glaze across the world
over the bald spot
of the tallest man
over the top
of the smallest coffin
and the shiny shanks
of your Sunday shoes

It's whatever we touch
and later scatter

How can so little matter
matter so much

Fadeout in ten
nine eight

13
So easy to lose
your place in the open-
ended story written with your breath

to be continued to be
told in wind across a field
through a latticework of trees

rewritten in the night
branch by branch
and on the page below you

the closing of the book
is not the ending of the story
now everywhere you look it is

seven   six   five

to be continued and continues
to be told in the curvature of hills
through which a stream is coursing

into your wounds the salve
of the world gliding
your way glacial as recovery

14
Breath   everything is riding on it
          under the door winter slides
its white envelope   past due past due

four   three   two

          as we move from bed to chair
and room to room   our lives
          sighing in the cedars

strung on backroads to this place
        where we go in and out
breath by breath   gravel and ice

        underfoot   Orion overhead

15

Standby
Cue reader
Reader go

In grandma's rocker
the envelope
of your lower back

            opens its
            triangular flap
            a letter falls out

                    sh-h-h-h-h-h-h
                    with the mantra
                    of the cottonwood

a glossy drop
of honeysuckle
on the tongue

            the scent of lilacs
            and a summer
            night on the dock

                    the lake pushing back
                    from its black lap
                    bones   shoes

worn like the unknown
remembered paths
behind the waist

        sealed over and over
        an unread letter
        like the one lone shutter

one

                banging all night in the wind
                Dear One   it begins   *I am here*
                Dear One   it goes on   *I never left*

one

I am who   *Dear One*   it ends
you always were
I am you who never left

one

        I am you who   *I am who you*
        never left   *always were*
        sorry forgive sorry   forgive sorry forgive

16
I've been with you
all this time more
than your mother
father longer
than your life-
long mate your kids
been with you
thick in sickness thin
in health till death
do you sweetly in
sorrow which breath
will be the last this

one or the one
just after
all we have
undergone what's
not to love

17
The light flares and dims
            branches stir inside the breath

after the flame   smoke
            scrawls its last line on the air

the cardinal returns after the mower passes
            the book of your body closes

as you lay it slowly down *goodbye!*
            on the bed you learned to make as a child

on the floor the cat once sailed
            on a raft of sunlight

on the bookshelf next to those
            whose names begin where yours left off

                                        Curtain

18
chills up the back
        of the arms
chills up the back
        of the legs the chills

that turn the skin
    to tiny mountains everywhere
turn the hair
    to pine forest

at the treeline you are waiting

coming   overcoming
chills on the hour
    from the bell tower
chills at the long
    forgotten song
chills at the unexpected
    moon pushing its head
    through a cloud
news on its way
    through you a humming
in the hands the phone
    ringing up your spine
    and out the crown
chills at the lights going down
chills at the curtain
    rising and the curtain
falling over and over
a reversal of snow
    dissolving upward
as time lifts its roof
    and there you go
rising like foam
the fizz of a girl you knew
    out the top of the turret
a frothing of who
you were   *br-r-r-r-r-r*
your footprints so far
    below

19

Rewriting the body
    its lines streaming out
        beyond the margins

the satin bookmark
    slipping through your fingers
        sliding down the spine

and out of the story
    lifted by a distant wind
        into your breath and mine

intermingled from the start
    and beyond the finish
        line the body rewritten

in another language
    in one ear out the other
        so suddenly soon

in the mind of another
    raising an eyebrow
        across the room

ACKNOWLEDGMENTS

Thanks to the editors of the following publications where versions of these poems first appeared:

Journals

The Common	"The Blue Hat"
	"Waiting for the Call"
	"First Kiss"
I-70 Review	"The Failing Heart"
	"Night Wine"
	"Snow Angel"
	"A Perfect Death"
The Journal	"In Extremis"
	"A Changing View"
Konza	"Driving Kansas"
The Midwest Quarterly	"Rewriting the Body"
New Letters	"Meanwhile You While He"
Nimrod	"After You Died"
	"Knowing the Difference"
North American Review	"Defending the Fort"
	"The Fitting Room"
	"Leaving Home"
	"Rejection Slip"
Pleiades	"Day After"
Poetrybay	"One House"
	"The Library"
	"The Lesson"
Prairie Schooner	"Walking Water"
	"Black Wedding Train"
	"Sweeping the Porch"
The Yale Review	"Pentimento"

Anthologies

Poetry & the Creative Mind (Academy of American Poets, 2017):
"Walking Water"
Kansas Time & Place: An Anthology of Heartland Poetry (Little Balkans Press, 2017):
"Force of Nature"
To the Stars Through Difficulties (Mammoth Publications):
Section 14, "Rewriting the Body"

GRATITUDE

Special thanks to j.m.rees, designer of worlds and words, for his inspired arrangements of "Song of Myself" and "The Back of Beyond."

Thanks to Humanities Kansas for their support throughout my term as Poet Laureate of Kansas, during which much of this book was written. Deep appreciation to Governor Kathleen Sebelius and the extinct Kansas Arts Commission for establishing the post—and to Caryn Mirriam-Goldberg for seeing it to shore in a storm of politics: a win/win for the state and the state of poetry.

Special thanks to Faith Shearin for her generous way-showing and to all who helped steer this endeavor in the direction of daylight: Kimberly Verhines, Sarah Denise Johnson, Helen Houghton, Jo McDougal, Eric McHenry, Colette Inez, and William Trowbridge. Thanks to the Heartland Writers, led by the fearless Judy Hyde, and to the Friday Writers.

Thanks to Fred Buchholz, creator of special effects for motion pictures, for lending his technical expertise to the title poem.

Gratitude to Pennie Cohn for love and insight, to Cindy Sullivan for climbing my tree, and to Susan and Tim Norris, accomplices extraordinaire.

A bow to my Yoganetics students, who teach me. Thanks to Unity Church of Overland Park for ongoing inspiration, and for hosting my yoga studio for the last quarter-century.

Thanks to Grace and Spencer Townley-Lott for their imaginative counsel and unfailing support, and to Russell Baker for his translation skills from legalese to English.

No thanks could encompass my gratitude for Roderick Townley, my favorite author, finest editor, and soulmate, for the love and steadfast presence that permeate my life.

ABOUT THE AUTHOR

Rewriting the Body is the sixth book from Wyatt Townley, Poet Laureate of Kansas Emerita. Other poetry collections include *The Afterlives of Trees*, *The Breathing Field*, and *Perfectly Normal*. Her work has been read by Garrison Keillor on NPR, selected by Ted Kooser for "American Life in Poetry," and published in journals from *The Paris Review* to *Newsweek*.

Wyatt has lived a double life as a poet and dancer, and her poetry drops anchor in the body—or body writ large in landscape and weather. She is the founder of Yoganetics®, a therapeutic yoga system borne of a serious spinal injury, now practiced on six continents. HarperCollins published her book on the method, selected an "Editor's Choice" by *Yoga Journal*.

The confluence of poetry and poetry-in-motion has shaped Wyatt's life.

www.WyattTownley.com

CPSIA information can be obtained
at www.ICGtesting.com
Printed in the USA
LVHW03s2051031018
592317LV00004B/6/P